Eucharistic Rosary

Eucharistic Rosary

Alan Ames

The decree of the Congregation of the Propagation of the Faith, A.A.S 58, 1186 (approved by Pope Paul VI on October 14, 1966) states that the Nihil Obstat and Imprimatur are no longer required on publications that deal with private revelations, provided that they contain nothing contrary to faith and morals.

The publisher recognizes and accepts that the final authority regarding the events described in this book rests with the Holy See of Rome, to whose judgement we willingly submit.

Sections of this book
may not be copied without
permission of the author.

© 2023 — Carver Alan Ames
Touch of Heaven
(Alan Ames Ministry)
PO Box 85
Wembley, 6014
West Australia

ISBN: 979-8-9893243-0-9

Contents

- 7   Foreword
- 8   About Alan Ames
- 10   How the Lord gave the Eucharistic Rosary
- 13   Joyful Mysteries
- 23   Luminous Mysteries
- 33   Sorrowful Mysteries
- 43   Glorious Mysteries
- 52   Our Lady's Promises
- 54   The Holy Trinity Rosary
- 57   Mary, Queen of the Cross
- 62   Healings

Foreword

By Beatrix Zureich

In October 2000, St. John Paul II. entrusted the whole world and the 3rd millennium to Our Lady, as he, with thousands of bishops and faithful, said the prayer of consecration in front of the statue of Our Lady of Fatima. In Fatima, Our Lady had asked for the rosary to be prayed, linking this to great promises.

Many people, even saints like St. Therese the Little Flower, had or have problems praying the 50 Hail Mary's. The mystery of the rosary is that it should be prayed while meditating on it, much more with the heart than with the mind. But how to do that? The Australian mystic Alan Ames gave an answer during one of his talks: We are to walk through the life of Jesus on this earth 2000 years ago, holding on to the hand of Our Lady and Jesus – how have the disciples, the soldiers, Mother Mary experienced each station in Jesus' life? If you put yourself into the life of Jesus in this way, you will discover the beauty of praying the rosary in a new way.

Alan received a new way of meditating the mysteries of the rosary through visions that point to the intimate relationship between the rosary and the holy eucharist. For each decade, he was given a vision as it is displayed hereinafter. For further immersion, we added a meditation to each decade, taken from the messages to Alan Ames. May this Eucharisic Rosary draw many graces upon those praying it!

About Alan Ames

Carver Alan Ames was born in England in 1953. In his youth, he lost the faith and got into bad company. He led a life full of violence, alcohol and sin. He married Kathryn and moved to Australia where the family settled down with two children. In 1993, his life came to a turning point when Alan suddenly heard an angel's voice. He started having visions and locutions of several saints and angels who asked him to change his life radically in order not to be lost forever.

During that time he experienced a "mini judgment", seeing the sins of his past life and how Jesus had suffered for each of these sins on the cross. That was the hardest and at the same time the most beautiful day of his life as Alan fell totally in love with Jesus.

Archbishop Barry Hickey from Perth (Western Australia) gave Alan a spiritual director who checks all the supernatural phenomena and to whom Alan is completely obedient. Since 1994, Alan has been giving his conversion testimony all over the world. With the explicit permission of his archbishop, after giving his talk, Alan prays especially for the sick for healing of body and soul. Alan is called to bring the love of God to people through all his charisms because God loves each and everyone.

The fruits of this ministry are conversions, healings and a rekindled love of the sacraments, especially of the holy eucharist and confession.

Through Alan Ames' example, God shows that it is never too late to repent and that God wants to embrace even the biggest sinner – all they need to do is to want God's forgiveness and to embrace it.

How the Lord gave the Eucharistic Rosary

By Alan Ames

After my conversion I had started to pray the rosary daily and to go to holy Mass every day. Then a very difficult time came that lasted for about two or three weeks. Within, I was struggling with perseverance in prayer. Then, just as I thought these dry times would never end and I would not be strong enough to go on, the most wonderful thing happened. On 30th June, 1995, Saint Raphael the Archangel spoke to me, saying:

"Under the emotional find the spiritual. When you find that you find the answer to eternal life. You must look with your spirit, not your eyes, and to look spiritually you must immerse yourself in prayer and meditation on the Most Holy Sacrament of the Eucharist.

Open your mind with deep thought on the mystery of the Lord's Body on the Most Holy Food of Communion.

Open your heart by letting that overwhelming feeling of love engulf you – do not block it, do not stop it, just let it flow through you. Open your spirit in the sacraments and open the way of letting God's gift to you become stronger. Do these things and grow in God's love. I give you my love and watch over you always. In God's name I bless you, and in God's name I offer you this help."

The next morning I had been to 8 o'clock Mass and was walking, praying the rosary, when at the end of the glorious mysteries, Jesus started speaking to me. The Lord said that He was going to give me a meditation on the rosary which was to be given to all, explaining later that it was:

1. For those who found it difficult to pray the rosary when the Blessed Sacrament was exposed.
2. For those who didn't pray the rosary as they thought they were praying to Our Lady, when in fact they were praying with Our Lady, to Jesus. It showed these people that the rosary centers around Jesus.
3. It was also for those who doubted the bread and wine of Communion is the Lord's Body and Blood.
4. For those who found it difficult at times to pray the rosary; this would help as it is a simple, uncomplicated meditation.

Then the Lord gave me the following visions:

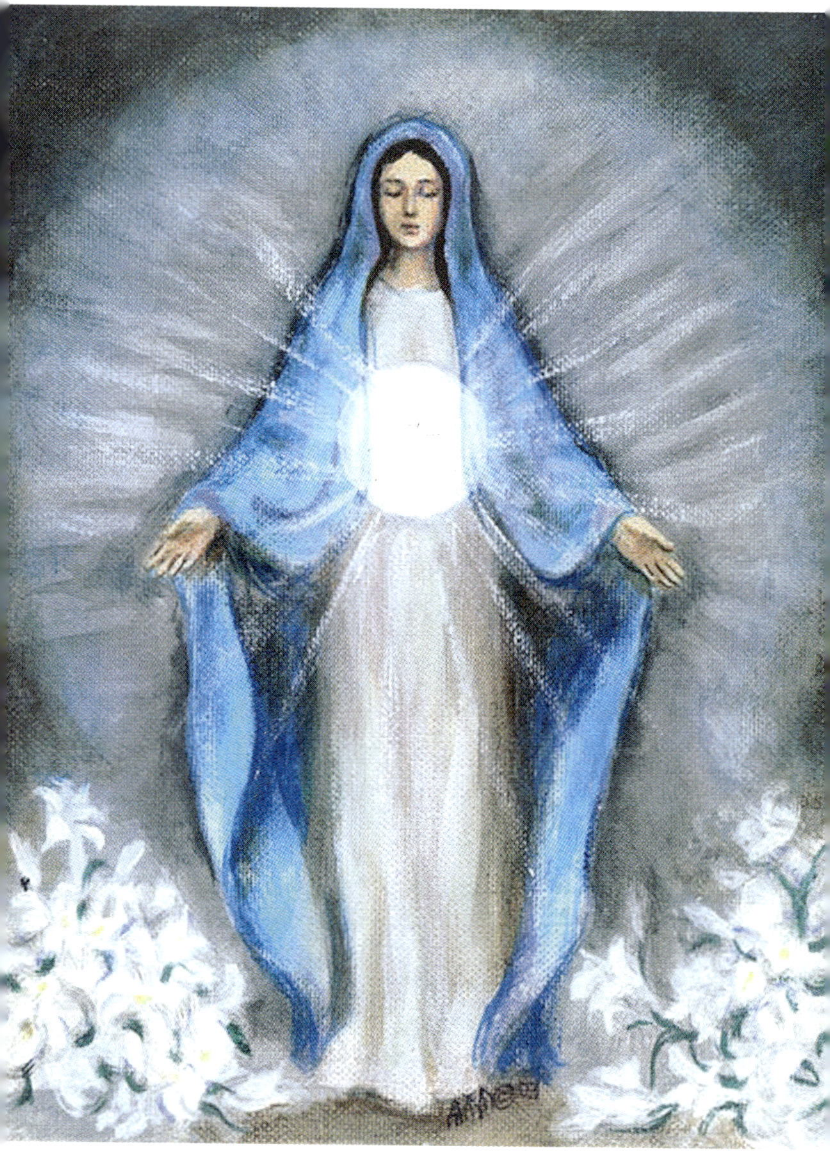

Joyful Mysteries

1st Mystery: *The Annunciation*

"Mary ... You are to conceive and bear a son, and you must name Him Jesus."
St. Luke 1:31

I saw Our Blessed Mother dressed in blue with the Host inside her body and the Host was shining bright.

Meditation:

Place your thoughts in my hands, place your love in my heart, and place your spirit in my spirit – and I will give them to my son Jesus as a gift.

Lay your heart on me, lay your life on me, lay yourself on me and I will comfort you, my dear son.

Caress my love with your soul, caress my soul with your love and become one with me in Jesus.

Falling down in adoration, falling down in love, falling down in delight, falling down in the arms of Jesus.

Our Lady, 29th December, 1994

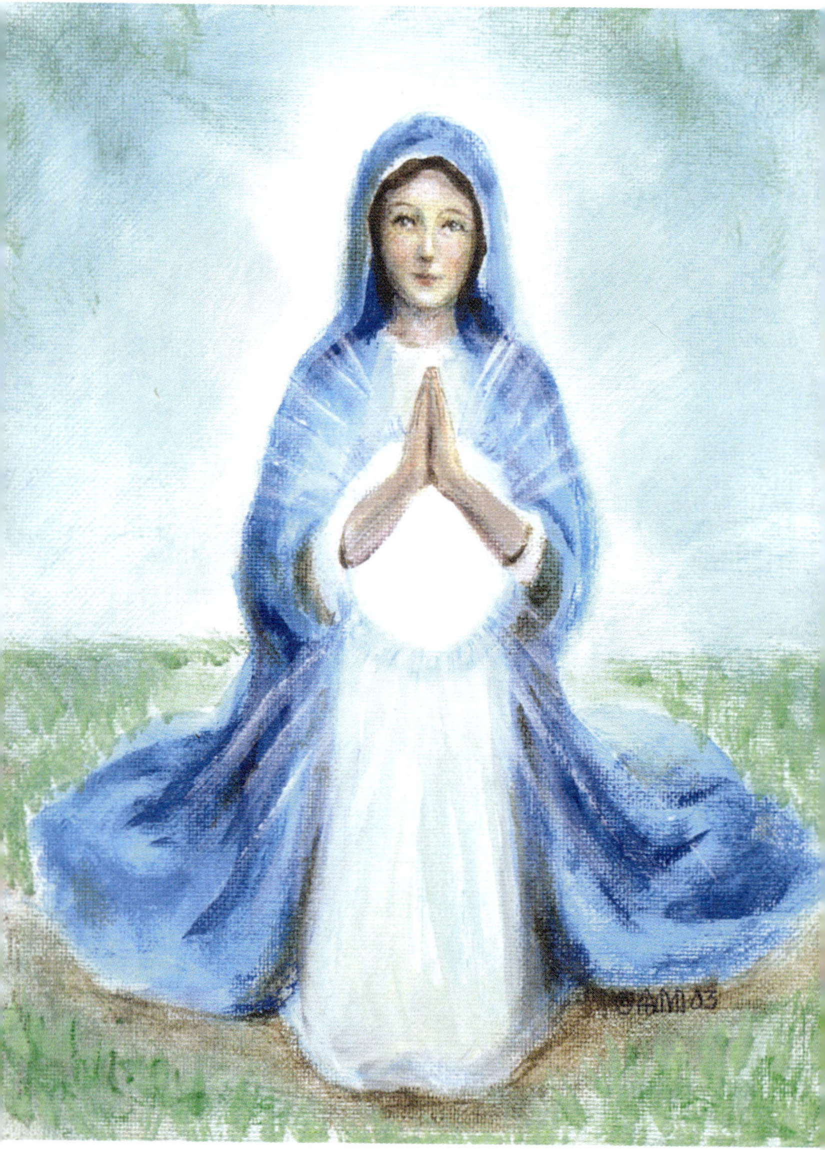

2nd Mystery: *The Visitation*

"Of all women you are the most blessed, and blessed is the fruit of your womb."
St. Luke 1:41

Our Mother, still in blue, had the Host within her body but now, as well as the Host shining white, so was Mother Mary. The words "My soul magnifies the Lord" were heard.

Meditation:

My dear children,
embrace Me in love,
embrace Me in joy,
embrace Me in the Eucharist.

Take Me within
and let Me fill you with My love.
Take Me within and let Me love you completely.
Take Me within and love Me.
The Lord Jesus, 27th October, 1994

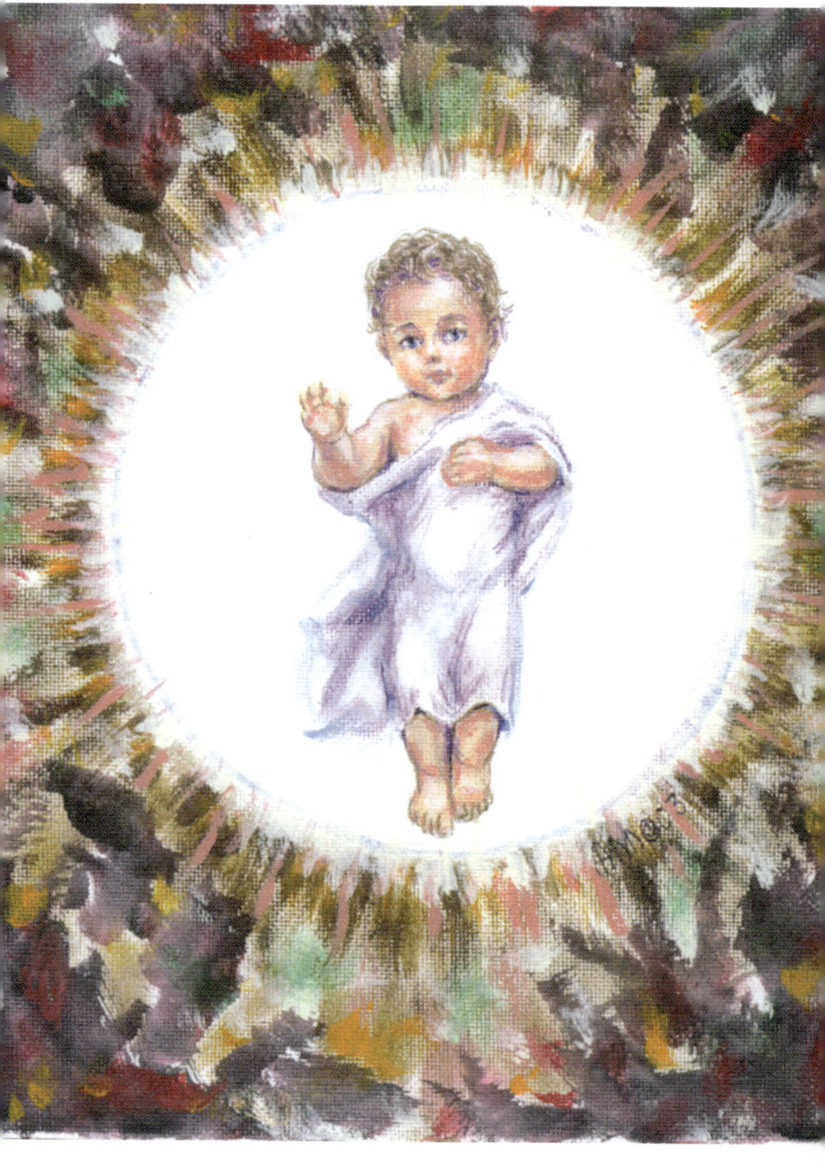

3rd Mystery: The Nativity

"Today in the town of David a saviour has been born – He is Christ the Lord."
ST. LUKE 2:11

The Host shining white and then Baby Jesus appeared in the middle.

Meditation:

When my Son was in my arms as a child and I held Him close to me, I could feel His love filling my very being. As He held onto my hand and squeezed it in an expression of His love, my heart was filled with joy. When He opened His eyes and looked into mine, His love penetrated my very soul. When He snuggled into my embrace, His love opened my heart to God.

This is how it should be every time you receive the Eucharist; you should accept and welcome the love of Jesus.
OUR LADY, 28TH JANUARY, 1995

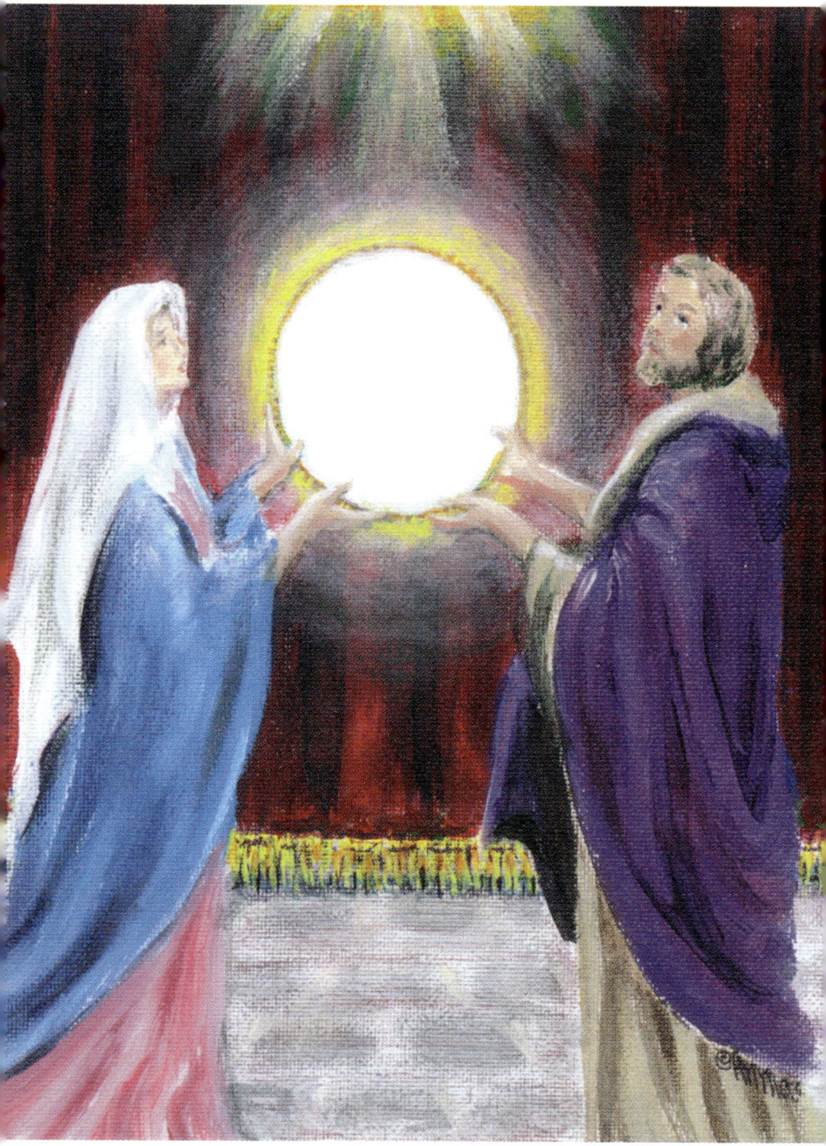

4th Mystery: *The Presentation*

"They took Him up to Jerusalem to present Him to the Lord."
ST. LUKE 2:22

Mother Mary and St. Joseph in the temple and between them they were holding the Host up high saying, "Father, this is Your Son."

Meditation:

Place your soul in My hands,
place your future in My hands
and place your destiny in My hands
and live forever.
THE LORD JESUS, 12TH NOVEMBER, 1994

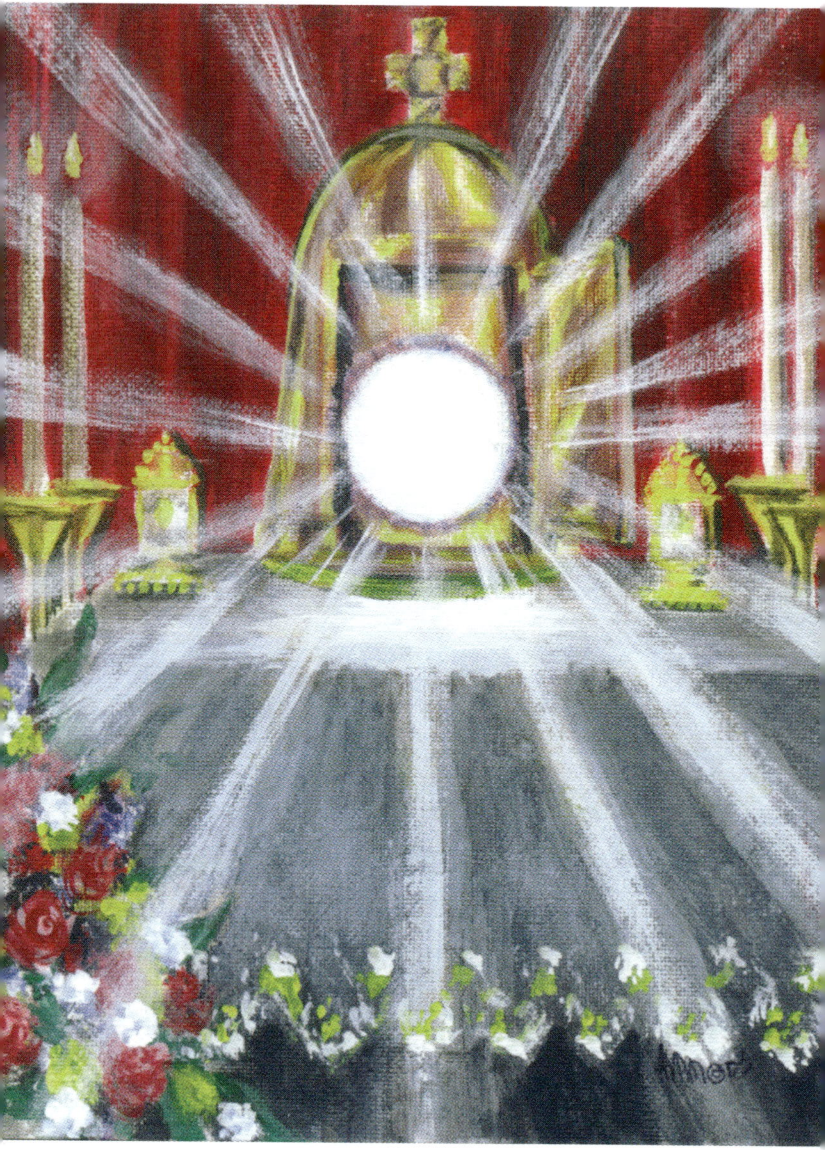

5th Mystery: Finding the Child Jesus in the Temple

"They found Him in the Temple."
St. Luke 2:46

The Tabernacle within a church was wide open; inside was the Host shining white. Jesus said, "Where else would you find Me, but in My Father's House?"

Meditation:

The strength you seek you will find in the Eucharist.
The love you need you will find in the Eucharist,
and the joy you desire you will find in the Eucharist,
for I am the Eucharist.
The Lord Jesus, 4th May, 1995

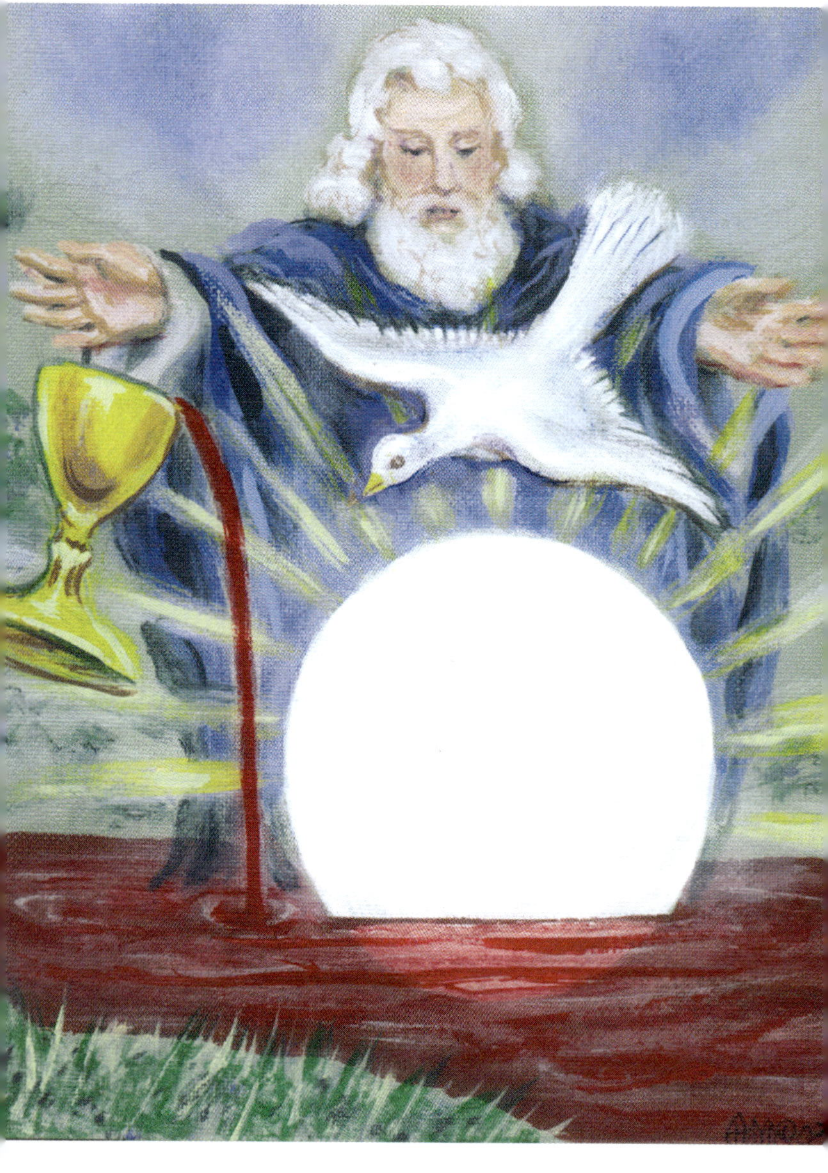

Luminous Mysteries

1st Mystery: The Baptism in the Jordan

"This is My beloved Son."
ST. MATTHEW 3:17

The gold chalice with blood flowing over the side to form a river of blood with a brightly shining Host descending into it and a white dove above the Host, and above the dove was the Father with His arms open wide. He was saying, "Come and bathe in the river of life."

Meditation:

In baptism, you are sealed in Jesus.
In baptism, you are made Mine.
In baptism, you are filled with the Spirit.

A soul consecrated to God,
A body given in love,
A child offered eternity.

Jeremiah 52:20 – Made for the house of the Lord.
GOD THE FATHER, 11TH AUGUST, 1997

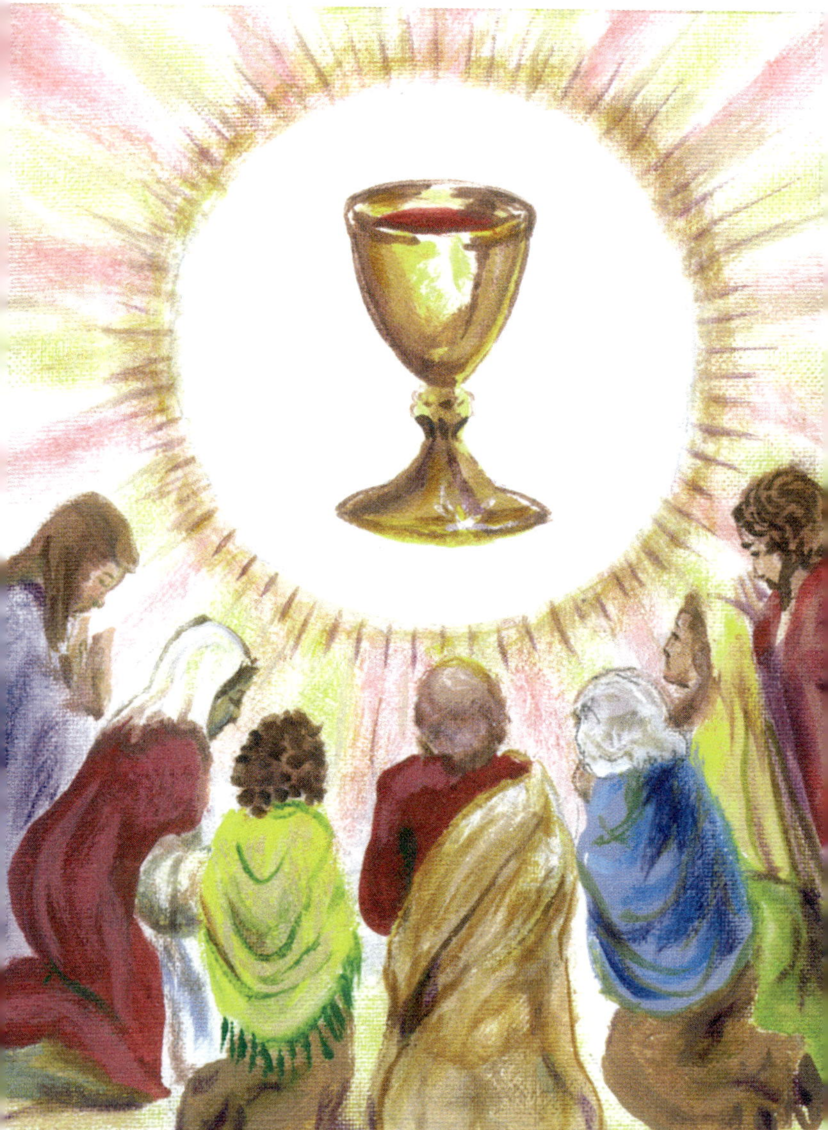

2nd Mystery: *The Wedding at Cana*

"You have kept the good wine until now."
St. John 2:10

The chalice inside the Host with the wedding guests all around it kneeling and praying. I heard the words, "By Your goodness we have this wine to offer."

Meditation:

When My Son offers you His love,
all He asks in return is your love.

When My Son offers you His heart,
all He asks in return is your heart.

When My Son offers you His life,
all He asks in return is your life.

What He offers is a love-filled life in His heart,
and all you need to do is return to Him.

Proverbs 3:5 – Trust in the Lord with all your heart.
God the Father, 4th September, 1997

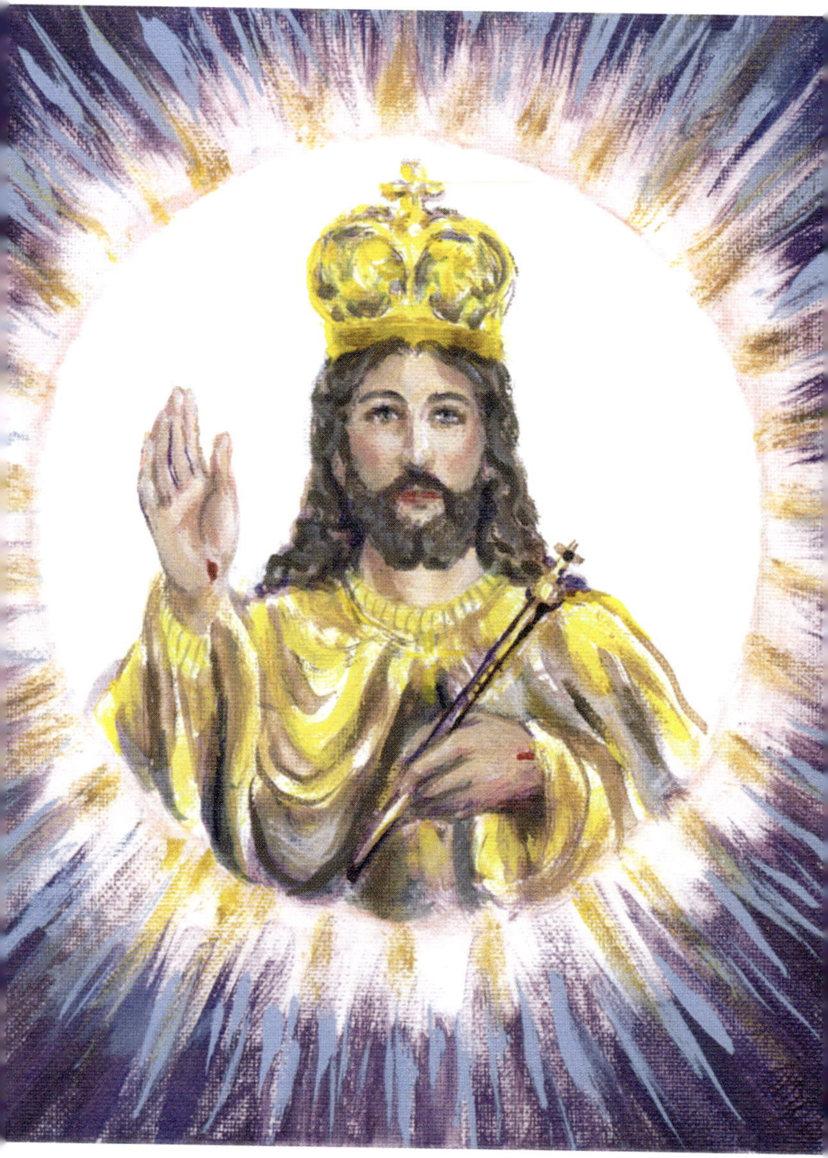

3rd Mystery: The Proclamation of the Kingdom of God

"Yet know this, the kingdom of God is at hand."
ST. LUKE 10:11

Inside a shining Host was Jesus crowned as King, dressed in gold, saying, "Here is the Kingdom."

Meditation:

The reign of peace will come to earth when all of mankind accepts Jesus as their king.

Acts 15:17 – Even all the Gentiles.
GOD THE FATHER, 22ND NOVEMBER, 1998

Would you see a man without food starve?
Would you see a man without drink thirst?
Would you see a man without love alone?

Those who do not love My Son, Jesus, are alone in the wilderness starving and dying of thirst.

Bring them the food they need to live, bring them the drink they need to survive, and bring them the love they need to be saved...bring them Jesus.

Hosea 11:4 – Stooping down to him, I gave him his food.
GOD THE FATHER, 14TH MARCH, 1997

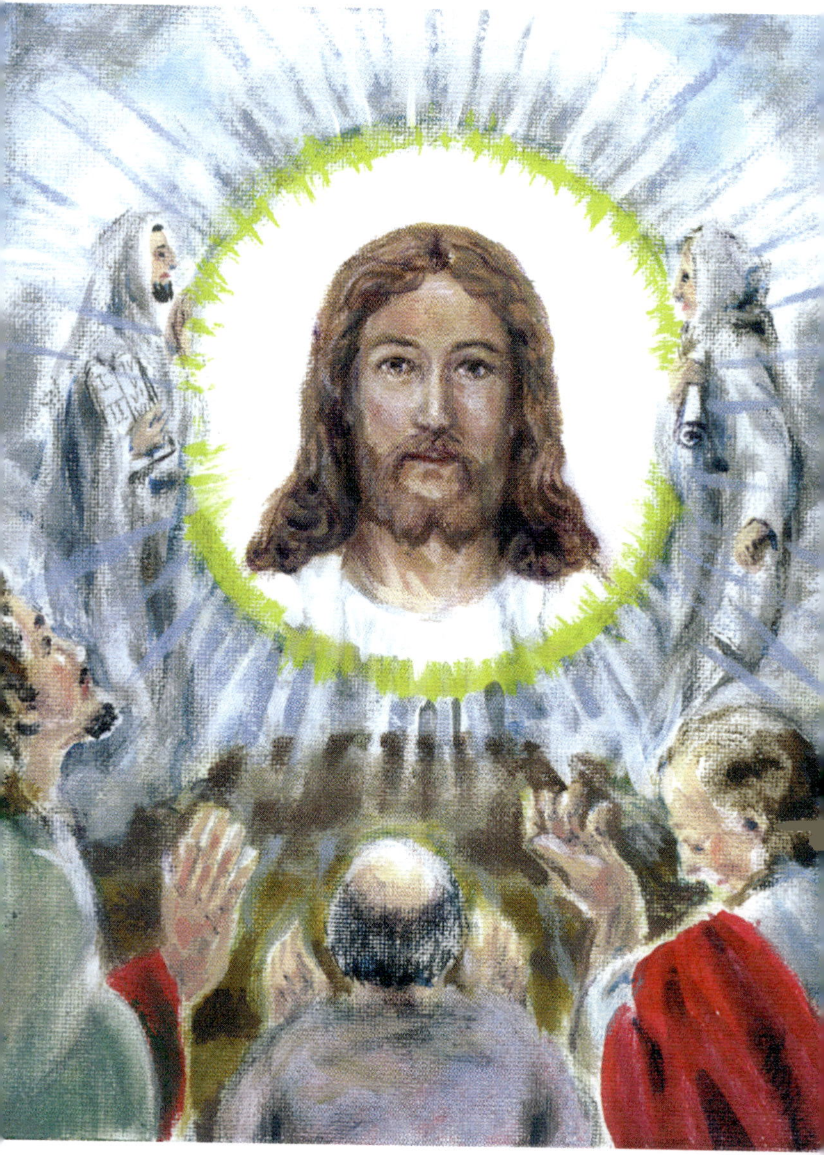

4th Mystery: *The Transfiguration*

"While He was praying His face was changed in appearance."
ST. LUKE 9:29

The Host was shining white with the face of Jesus in it and Jesus saying, "Be changed in Me."

Meditation:

In the Bread of Life, find Jesus.
In Jesus, find life.

In the Wine of Forgiveness, find Jesus.
In Jesus, find forgiveness.

In the Bread and Wine of Communion, find Jesus' forgiving love, which brings true life.

St. Luke 18:30 – In the world to come, eternal life.
GOD THE FATHER, 20TH MAY, 1996

The face of love, the face of Jesus.
The face of mercy, the face of Jesus.
The face of God, the face of Jesus.
GOD THE FATHER, 15TH SEPTEMBER, 1996

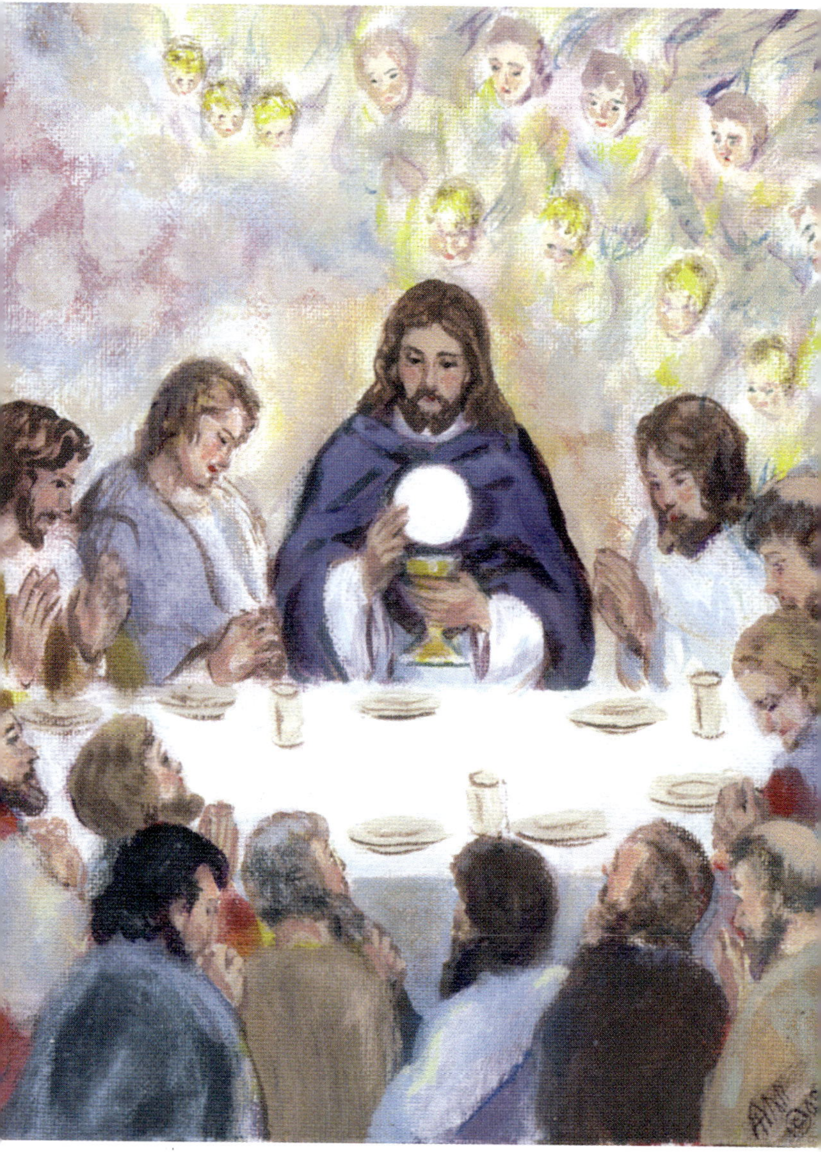

5th Mystery: *The Institution of the Eucharist*

"The new covenant."
ST. LUKE 22:20

Jesus dressed in purple robes of a priest, holding a Host in one hand and a chalice in the other, standing at the altar with the apostles around it. He said, "This is My Body... this is My Blood."

Meditation:

In the Eucharist place your soul,
and then in your soul, find peace.

1 John 3:24 – From the spirit that He gave us.
GOD THE FATHER, 29TH DECEMBER, 1997

When you feel tired, rest.
When you feel lost, pray.
When you feel empty, receive the sacraments.

The tiredness, emptiness, and feeling lost are all signs that you are in need of My strength, found through prayer and the sacraments.
GOD THE FATHER, 1ST MARCH, 1996

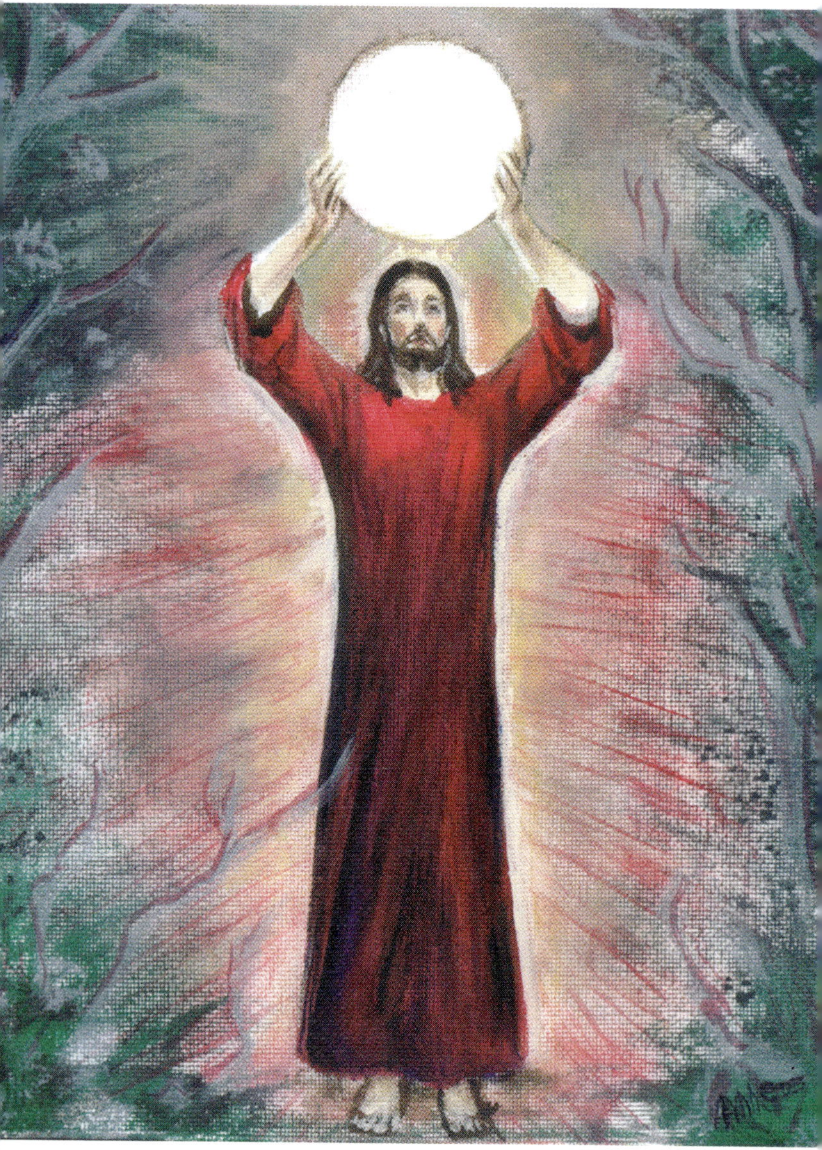

Sorrowful Mysteries

1st Mystery: *The Agony in the Garden*

"Father, let Your will be done, not Mine."
St. Luke 22:43

Jesus dressed in a red robe was holding the Host high above His head saying, "Father, this is My Body, I offer it to You, Your will be done."

Meditation:

A step along the path to Heaven is never easy, each step is a struggle with yourself and each step is a fight with evil.

When you overcome yourself you overcome evil, when you overcome your weakness you overcome evil and when you overcome your sin you overcome evil.

Then the steps to Heaven become clearer, simpler to follow but still hard to walk.

The Lord Jesus, 26th January, 1995

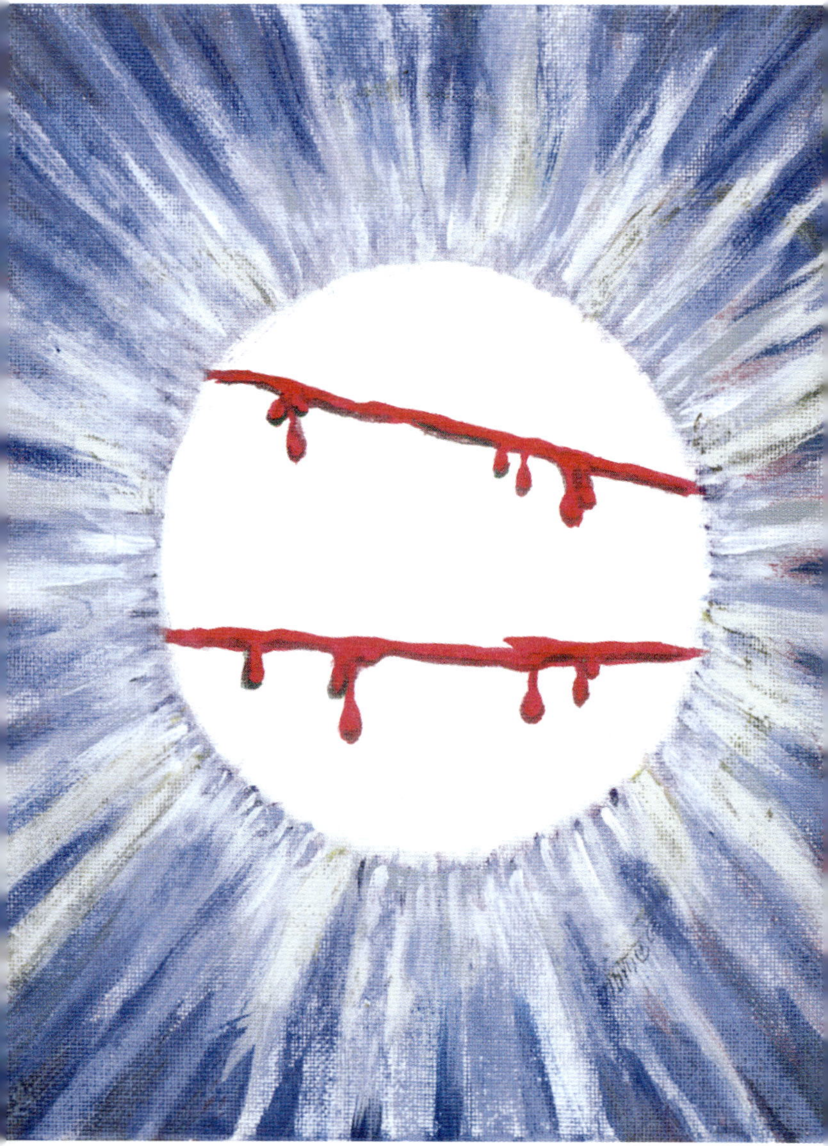

2nd Mystery: The Scourging

"Pilate then had Jesus taken away and scourged."
St. John 19:2

The Host was shining white and with each stroke of the whip a red line appeared across it and the Host started to bleed.

Meditation:

When you look upon the Body of Jesus in the sacrament of the Eucharist, see His love.

When you look upon the Blood of Jesus in the sacrament, see His mercy.

When you look upon the bread, see the Body and Blood there for you, there in love and mercy.
God the Father, 17th August, 1995

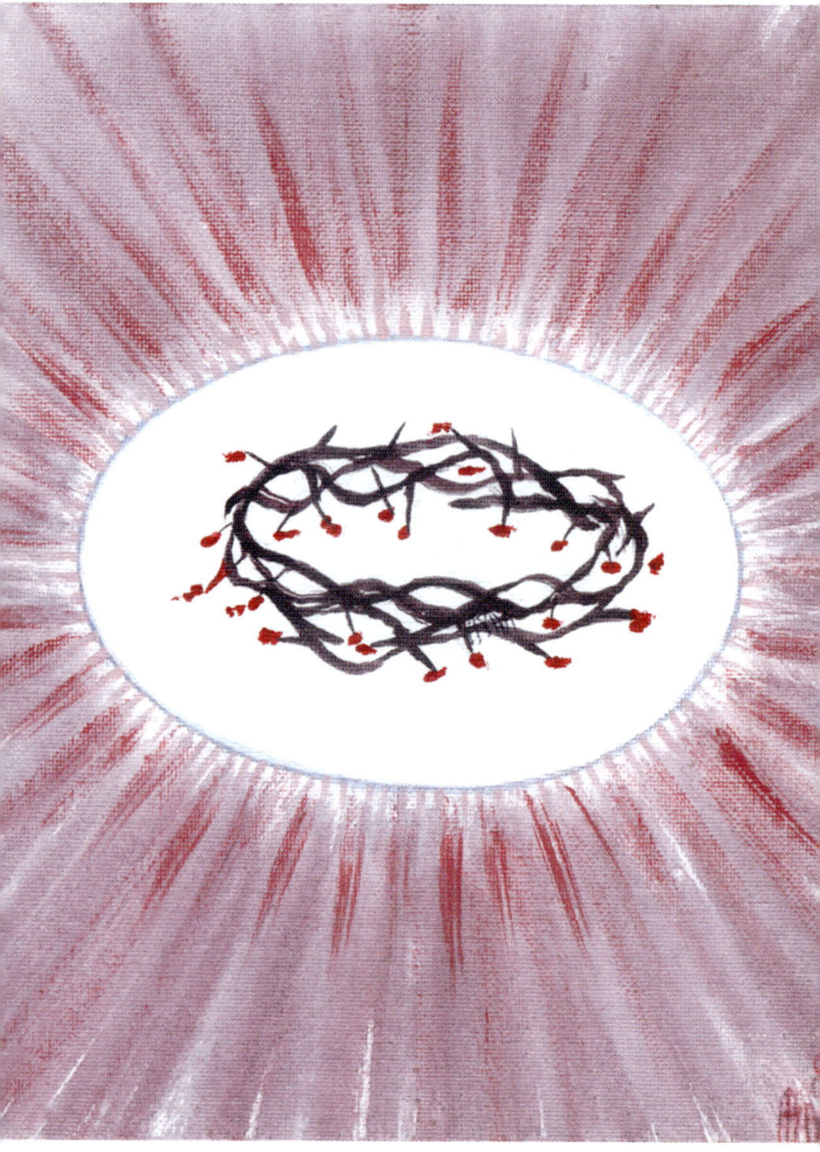

3rd Mystery: The Crowning with Thorns

"After this, the soldiers twisted some thorns into a crown and put it on His head."
ST. JOHN 19:2

The Host shining white was lying on its side as a crown of thorns descended upon it. As the thorns pierced the Host it started to bleed.

Meditation:

Thorns, nails and a spear could not stop My mercy, they magnified it.

Pain, suffering and humiliations cannot stop your work, they can only glorify it.

Love, faith and hope can strengthen your shoulders for the cross that you have to carry.

THE LORD JESUS, 27TH APRIL, 1995

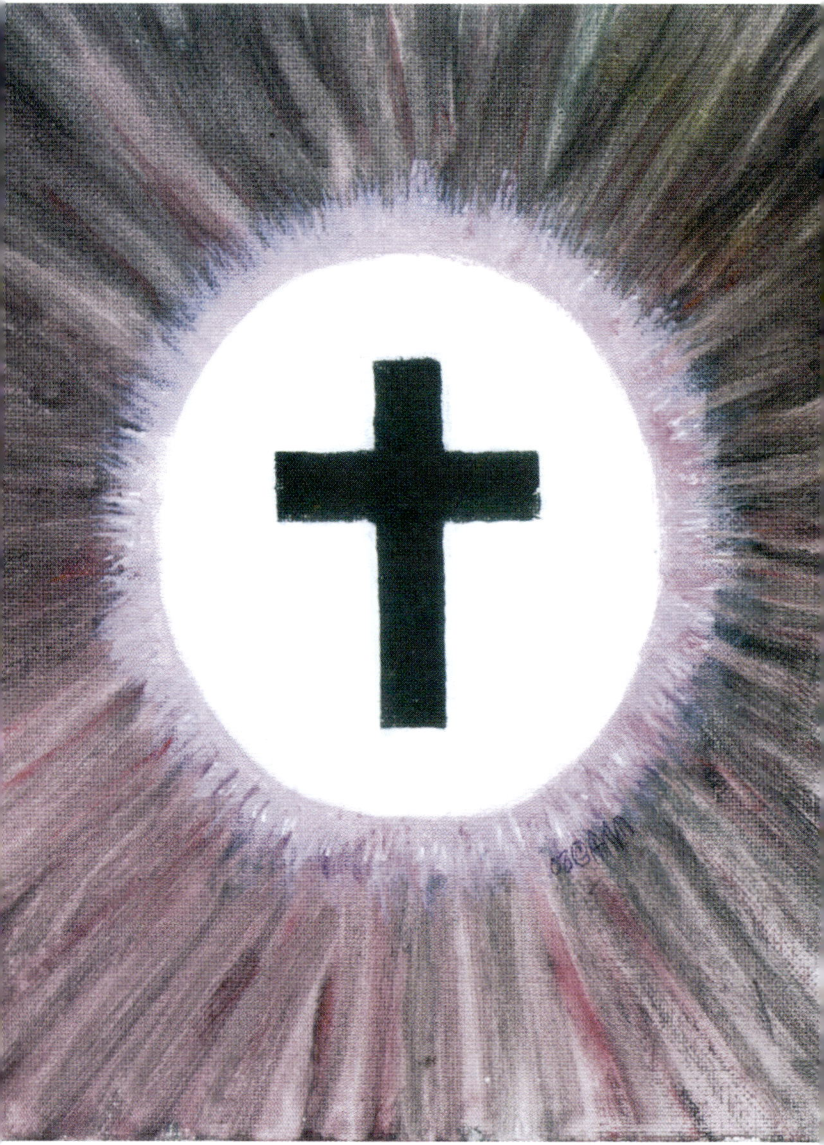

4th Mystery: *The Carrying of the Cross*

"Carrying His own cross, He went out of the city to the place of the skull ... Golgotha."
St. John 19:17

The Host was shining white with a dark cross in the center. The cross got darker and the Host shone brighter. Jesus explained that with each step the cross became heavier, but with each step He glorified God.

Meditation:

As My Son Jesus carried the cross upon His shoulder, I wept tears of joy and tears of sorrow.

The joy that man's sins would be forgiven and that they would be welcomed in Heaven if they followed My Son's way.

The sorrow to see My sweet Son suffer so, to see Him treated as if He was a sinner, but how else to forgive sins except to take the pain for them.

God the Father, 3rd February, 1995

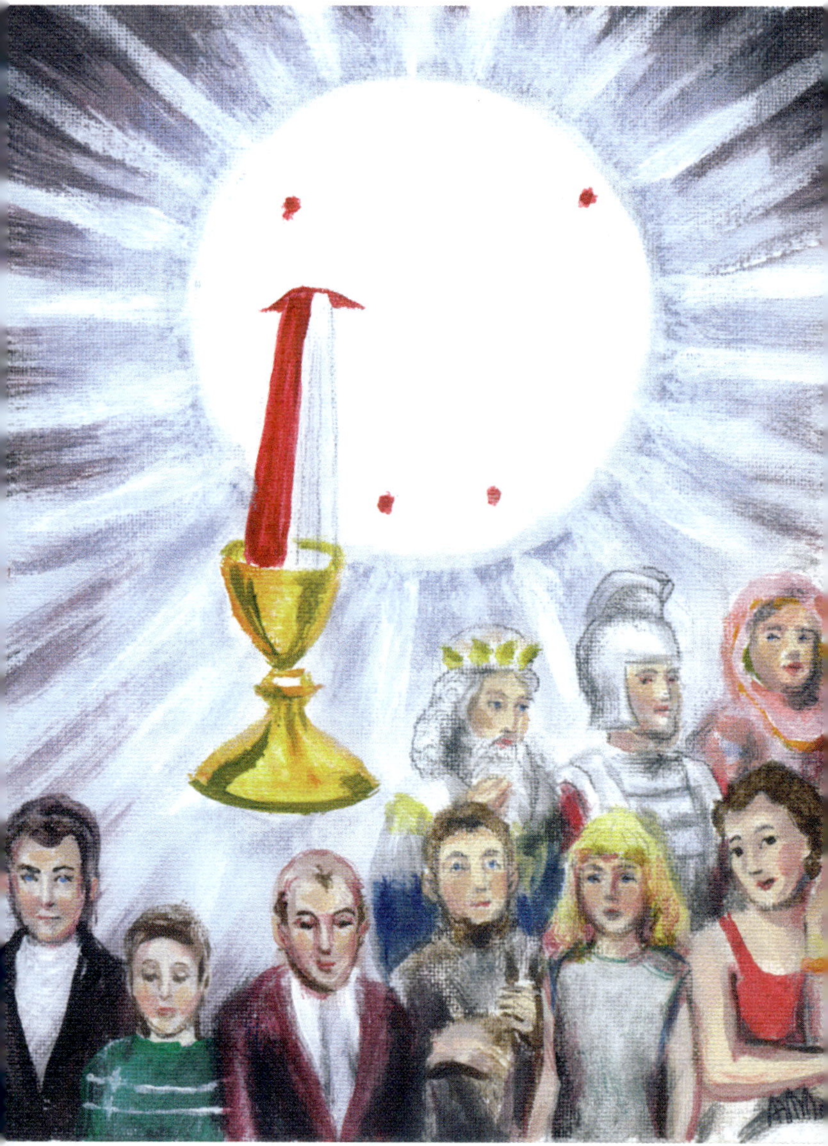

5th Mystery: The Crucifixion

"They crucified Him ... One of the soldiers pierced His side with a spear; and immediately there came out blood and water." – "After this, many of His disciples went back and walked no more with Him."
ST. JOHN 19:14,34 AND 6:67

The Host shining white had four wounds which were bleeding, then changed to be Jesus on the cross. When Jesus was on the cross, the Roman soldiers, the Pharisees and the Jews were turning their backs on Jesus saying, "This is not the Son of God." When it was the Host, it was the people of today turning their backs on the Host saying, "This is not the Body of Jesus." Then the Host was pierced with a spear and started to shed water and blood into a chalice.

Meditation:

Cross of Jesus, cross of Man.
Cross of Pain, cross of Sorrow.
Cross of Forgiveness, Cross of Redemption.
Cross of Love.
GOD THE FATHER, 12TH FEBRUARY, 1995

Jesus opened His arms on the cross
and embraced mankind with His love.
GOD THE FATHER, 29TH JANUARY, 1995

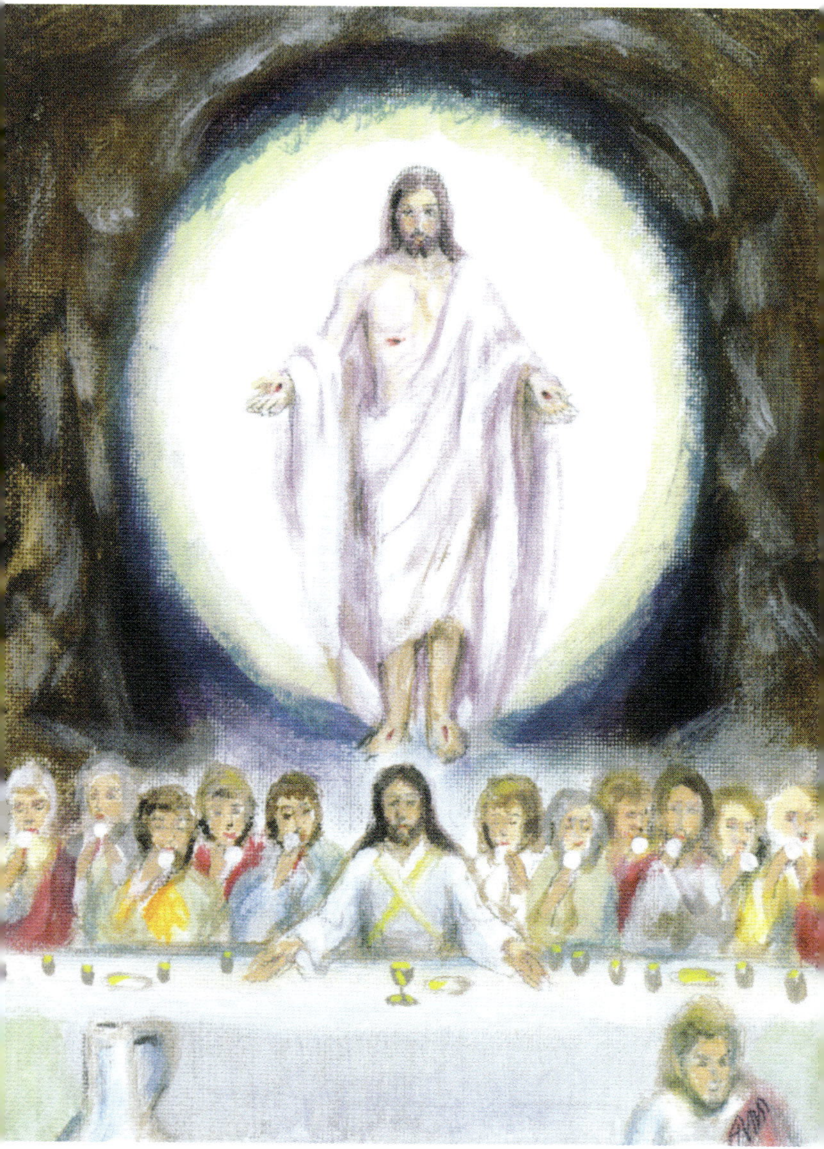

Glorious Mysteries

1st Mystery: The Resurrection

"Anyone who eats My flesh and drinks My blood has eternal life and I shall raise him up on the last day."
ST. JOHN 6:54

Jesus appeared within the Host at the entrance of the tomb, His arms open wide. Then Jesus was in a room with the apostles at a meal, each of whom was consuming a Host. Jesus said, "I am the Food of Life."

Meditation:

Taken within, the Host becomes
the Lord Jesus' healing power.

Taken within, the Host becomes
Jesus' healing love.

Taken within, the Host becomes one with you
and you become one with Jesus.
GOD THE FATHER, 5TH APRIL, 1995

The cross, the spear and the grave are signs that in God's love all can be overcome and that all is there, if only mankind would love God.
THE LORD JESUS, 22ND APRIL, 1995

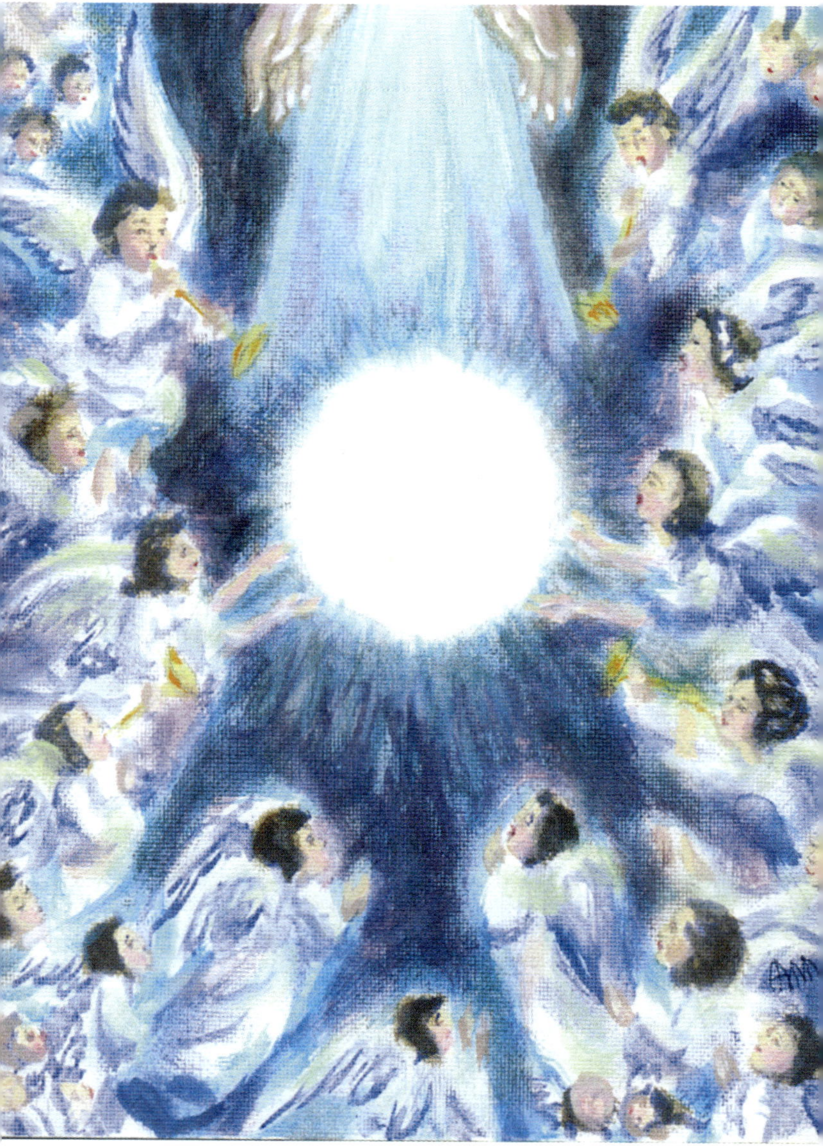

2nd Mystery: The Ascension

"Now as He blessed them, He withdrew from them and was carried up into Heaven."
ST. LUKE 24:51

There were hundreds and hundreds of angels flying around, some singing, some blowing trumpets. The angels had the Host between them and flew up to Heaven; the clouds parted and a white light shone down with the Father saying, "This is My Son."

Meditation:

Flights of Angels surround the Lord
singing His praise and glory.

Flights of Angels encompass the Lord
offering Him their love.

Flights of Angels together with the saints
fall in adoration of the Lord.

The joy in Heaven of the Lord's saving grace given to mankind knows no end, for all in Heaven want mankind with them in God's love.
OUR LADY, 19TH APRIL, 1995

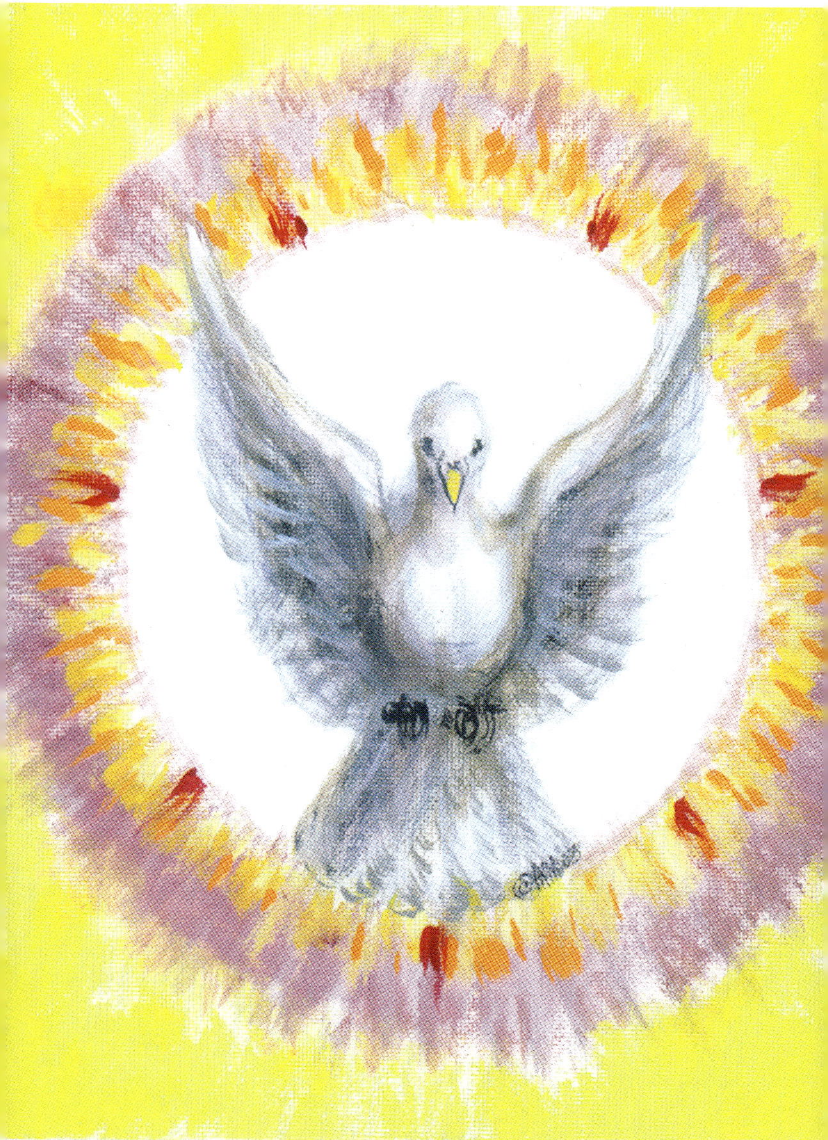

3rd *Mystery: The Descent of the Holy Spirit*

"This is the bread come down from heaven."

"Let Your Spirit come down upon these gifts to make them holy."
St. John 6:58 and Eucharistic Prayer II

The Host appeared shining white and a beautiful white dove formed in the Host. Jesus said, "When you receive Me, you receive the Holy Spirit."

Meditation:

Feel My love,
Feel My fire,
Feel My strength.

Feel My faith,
Feel My joy,
Feel My gifts.

Feel My truth,
Feel My light,
Feel My graces.

Feel them within and then share them without.
The Holy Spirit, 26th October, 1995

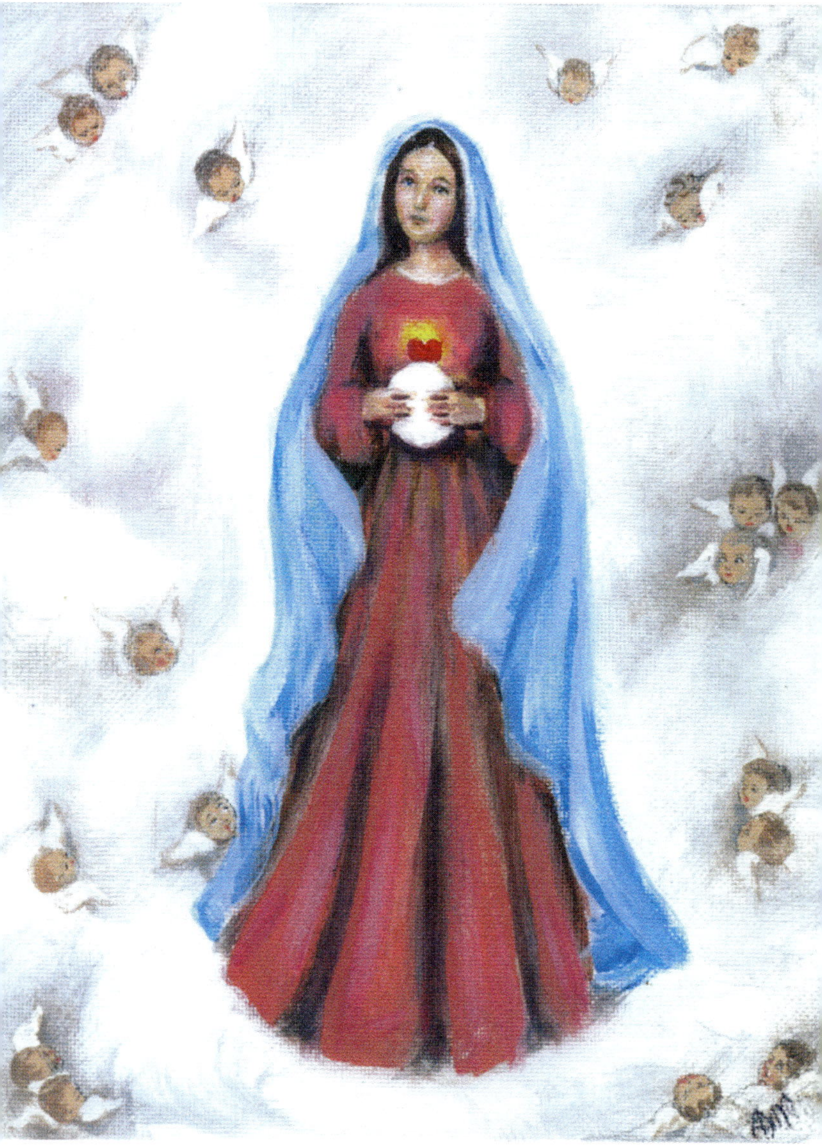

4th Mystery: *The Assumption*

"All powerful and everliving God, You raised the sinless Virgin Mary, mother of Your Son, body and soul to the glory of Heaven."

OPENING PRAYER – MASS OF ASSUMPTION

Our Blessed Mother appeared in Heaven with her Immaculate Heart exposed. In the middle of her heart was the Host shining white; Mother then embraced the Host.

Meditation:

Lifted to Heaven in love,
Lifted to Heaven in body,
Lifted to Heaven in God's glory.

When I was taken home to Heaven by my Son, it was a glorious day. I was filled with love throughout my body, and with this love I was assumed to the Father in Heaven.

OUR LADY, 15TH AUGUST, 1995

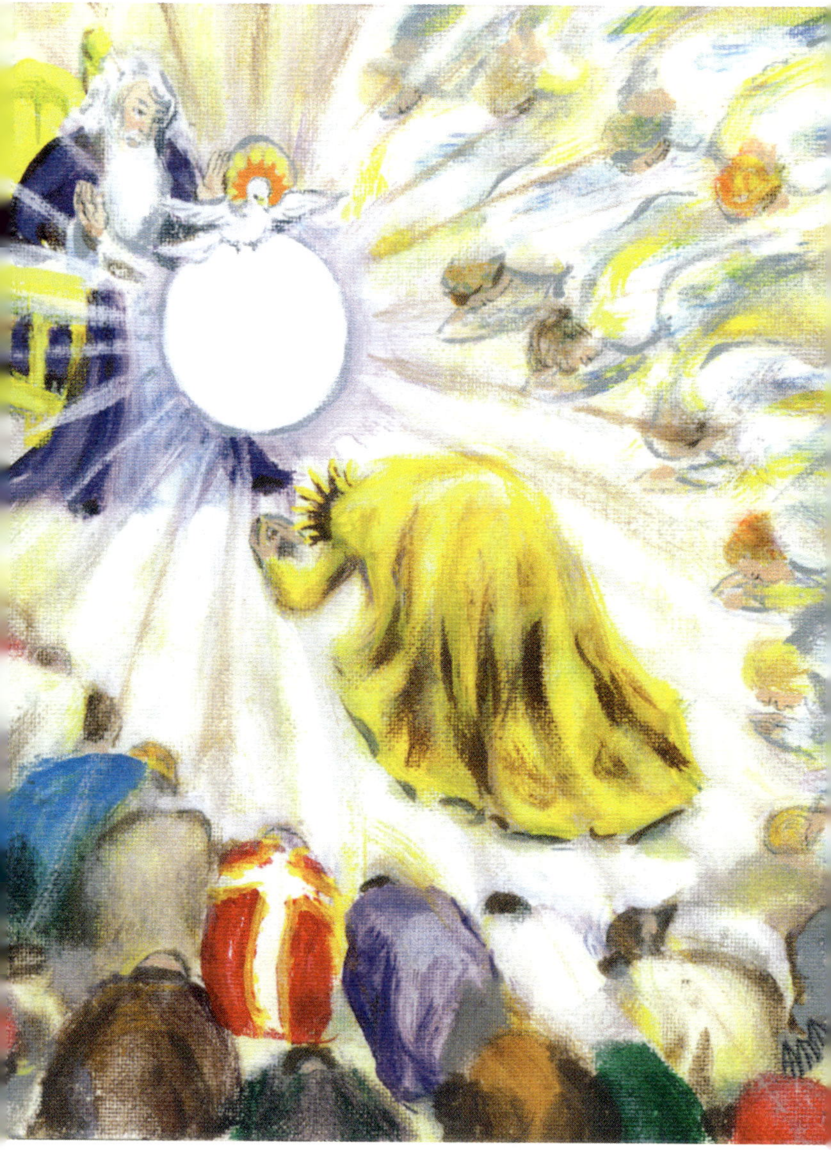

5th Mystery: The Coronation of Our Blessed Lady in Heaven as its Queen

"The Queen stands at Your right hand arrayed in gold."
PSALM 45:10

Mother Mary was dressed in gold with a golden crown as Queen of Heaven. In front of Mother was a large Host shining white with a dove flying around it. Behind the Host was the throne of the Father. Our Blessed Mother knelt towards the Host in humility facing the ground; behind her millions and millions of angels and saints did the same.

Meditation:

Bowing down before your God in adoration and worship is the most important act of love that you can offer Me. When you do this, you become Mine for eternity.
GOD THE FATHER, 24TH MARCH, 1995

In Mother's arms you will find love,
In Mother's heart you will find joy,
In Mother's soul you will find humility.
THE LORD JESUS, 1ST OCTOBER, 1995

Our Lady's Promises

By Alan Ames

When Jesus gave me the Eucharistic Rosary, He said, "This is the Eucharistic Rosary. It is for people having problems to pray the rosary when the Blessed Sacrament is exposed."

The Eucharistic Rosary is for those who think the rosary is prayed to Our Lady while in reality, we meditate with and through Our Blessed Mother on the Body, the Blood and the life of Jesus. We had a brochure done on the Eucharistic Rosary and when I was just speaking with those helping me about what we should do with it, Our Lady appeared to me. She had her hands cupped together holding colored rosaries. I saw the rosaries fall from her hands to all sides. Our Lady said, "Give a rosary with each booklet and I will bless this rosary."

Our Blessed Mother said also that the rosaries should first be blessed by a priest because the priests are so special. The priests' hands are consecrated. She showed this to me one day in the Cathedral of Perth where I live. The Blessed Sacrament had been exposed and in front of it there was a kneeler for the priest. The priest had not yet come when Our Blessed Mother appeared to me. I saw her kneel on the marble floor, so I said to her, "Why are you not kneeling on the kneeler on the cushion? It is much more comfortable there!" She replied, "No, this is for the priests, they are so special!"

Special things are happening with this rosary. For example, if you give it to people who are not praying the rosary, many of them start praying it. A grace is granted that many will pray the rosary. Sometimes it happens right away, other times it takes a while. It seems that through this rosary, special graces are also granted to families.

The Holy Trinity Rosary

After Our Blessed Mother Mary first appeared to me during 1993, she asked me to start praying more than the fifteen decades of the rosary which I was praying at that time. I did not know many other ways of praying, so Our Lady asked me to pray "The Trinity Rosary".

When asked why it contains no "Hail Mary's", she explained that this prayer was a special way of praising God. She said that she would join in prayer, with me and anyone else who prayed this rosary, whenever it was said, and we would praise God together. Our Mother said that when this rosary is prayed, it brings her great joy to see each soul praising the Holy Trinity.

I have found the Trinity Rosary has helped deepen my prayer life and I encourage those seeking a deeper spirituality to also pray it. The Trinity Rosary is a meditation on God that offers so many graces to those who pray it.

It can be prayed at any time, but I suggest that a very good time to pray the Holy Trinity Rosary is immediately after you complete your regular rosaries for the day.

On 8th August, 1996, Our Lady promised the following graces to those who recite this rosary:
1. Graces are granted through the Trinity Rosary for those in purgatory.
2. Graces are granted through the Trinity Rosary for those who suffer.

3. Graces are granted through the Trinity Rosary for those who want to come closer to God.

How to pray the Holy Trinity Rosary

This rosary starts immediately with the sign of the cross and:

11 "Our Father's" meditating on God the Father.
 1 "Glory Be" thinking of the Father in the Holy Trinity.

11 "Our Father's" meditating on the Lord Jesus.
 1 "Glory Be" thinking on Jesus in the Holy Trinity.

11 "Our Father's" meditating on the Holy Spirit.
 1 "Glory Be" thinking on the Holy Spirit in the Holy Trinity.

 1 "Hail Holy Queen" to finish, and the sign of the cross.

Vision on 23rd December, 1994

As I was praying the Holy Trinity Rosary on the plane, I had an inner vision. During the first 11 Our Father's I saw golden rays of light representing the Father. During the second 11 Our Father's I saw a golden crown of thorns which was Jesus and during the third 11 Our Father's I saw the golden flames of the Holy Spirit.

A golden spark rose from the flames and flew into my heart and soul, becoming a golden flame within me.

MARY QUEEN OF THE CROSS

Mary, Queen of the Cross

An artist painted this image of grace according to Alan's vision of Mary as the Queen of the Cross. The picture has already been spread far and wide, there are reports about prayers being heard and healings related to praying to Mary as the Queen of the Cross.

If you meditate on this painting in prayer, you might see that in the folds of Mary's garments a dove has formed. After that, the face of Jesus crucified was to be seen in Mary's right hand. In the clouds, sometimes also new images can be seen. Through this miraculous painting, God wants to speak to us through Mother Mary.

Below, you will find the messages relating to the painting:

Our Lady on 31st December, 1994
Red is the color of my Son's blood which was shed for mankind, red is the color of His love. As I stood by the cross, I shared in my Son's suffering and pain, I share in His love. White is the color of the water that flowed from His side, the water that washes man's sins away in love. As I stood by the cross I shared in the giving of this water.

Gold is the color of the cross, the cross of the King. Gold on my garment shows that I was with my Son on the cross.

The smile of love shows the deep love I have for my children, a mother's love.

The scapular shows mankind that my love can be attained by wearing my sign.

The rosary tells my children to pray and pray the rosary. It is through prayer that I lead you to Jesus.

My outstretched hand is there for my children to take so that I can walk with them to my Son Jesus.

My arms are opened to embrace my children in an eternal joining of our hearts to become one in Jesus.

I ask to be called Queen of the Cross because the Father has granted me the grace of sharing in the redemption of mankind with my Son Jesus who by His sacrifice has opened the door to Heaven to His children.

Jesus on 16th January, 1995
About the painting of the Queen of the Cross:

A painting of love, a painting of Mother.
A painting of giving, a painting of Mother.
A painting of offering, a painting of Mother.
A painting from Heaven, a painting of Mother.
A painting from God, a painting of Mother.
A painting from sanctity, a painting of Mother.
A painting for all, a painting of Mother.

Our Lady on 16th January, 1995
Nailed to the cross was my Son Jesus, pain filled His body and soul. As I watched, an agony within burned so deep I could not stand. On my knees I prayed and prayed, on my

knees I wept for my Son's agony to end and on my knees I saw the glory of God.

I saw how much God loves His children, how much He was prepared to give to save them and how much He needed to forgive them.

Nailed to the cross with my Son was my spirit, my being, my self. Nailed to the cross with my Son was my love, not as an equal but as a hand maiden wanting to serve her Lord and her God.

In the service of Jesus was I, as I watched His supreme act of love, a service I long all to share with me so they can find the rewards that await them in Heaven, the rewards of God.

Our Lady on 17th January, 1995
Queen of the Cross, Queen of Sorrow, Queen of Heaven. The cross and the sorrow show the way to Heaven and I as Queen lead to God.

Our Lady on 4th December, 1994
By the cross I stood and watched my Son Jesus give His life for man. I stood and prayed to the Father in Heaven to forgive them for what they did. I prayed to the Father to ease the pain of Jesus and I prayed for strength to see Jesus through this terrible suffering. With John at my side we offered all our love to the Father if He would ease the suffering just a little. We offered all of ourselves if He would lift this burden from the Messiah.

I knew He could not, for this sacrifice was needed to release man from his own chains, the chains that mankind had brought upon himself. I wanted to embrace my Son and comfort Him; I wanted to hold Him in my arms and tell Him I loved Him and His mother was there; I wanted to smother Him with affection as I did when He was a child.

I wanted my Son to live but I knew He could not, that He must endure death so that He could show how much God loves man. The tears of sorrow that ran from my eyes created pools of love, pools of motherly care and pools of everlasting joy. The heaviness of my heart created the love that I have for all mankind, created the special bond between myself and all of mankind.

Now I shed tears again as my foolish children follow the path of self destruction, follow the path of evil and sin. Do I have to have my heart broken again? Do I have to endure the sorrow that comes when a mother sees her children hurt themselves? Do I have to mourn again at the death of my children, a death that will last forever?

All I want for my children is goodness, all I want for my children is love, all I want for my children is Heaven; I want all for my children. If mankind can change now, if mankind can start to pray, to love God and each other, receive the sacraments often and live the life that God created them for, then and only then can this planet become the paradise it was meant to be. If mankind can learn to forgive, to accept others regardless of differences and become one family, the family of God, then and only then can eternity be theirs (in Heaven).

Prayer for Graces

If these prayers are said when holding my picture as Queen of the Cross in your heart, the person praying will be given a grace from God.

I ask the Lord to grant me through His Blessed Mother Mary, Queen of the Cross, this grace:

Mention what you are praying for. Say:
3 Hail Mary's
3 Our Father's and
3 Glory Be's.

Healings

There have been reported healings from praying the eucharistic rosary. Please report any healings to; email: alanames@alanames.org

Books available from:

USA
Alan Ames Ministry
PO Box 1281
Madisonville, Louisianna 70447

Web: http://www.alanames.org

Australia
Touch of Heaven
(Alan Ames Ministry)
PO Box 85
Wembley, 6014
West Australia

Phone: 61 89275 6608
Email: touchofheaven@iinet.net.au